BUDDHA
MEDITATIONS

THE ART OF LETTING GO

BUDDHA
MEDITATIONS

THE ART OF LETTING GO

Lisa TE Sonne

FALL RIVER PRESS

New York

Fall River Press

New York

An Imprint of Sterling Publishing
387 Park Avenue South
New York, NY 10016

ISBN 978-1-4351-4842-0

Distributed in Canada by Sterling Publishing
c/o Canadian Manda Group, 165 Dufferin Street
Toronto, Ontario, Canada M6K 3H6
Distributed in the United Kingdom by GMC Distribution Services
Castle Place, 166 High Street, Lewes, East Sussex, England BN7 1XU
Distributed in Australia by Capricorn Link (Australia) Pty. Ltd.
P.O. Box 704, Windsor, NSW 2756, Australia

For information about custom editions, special sales, and premium and corporate purchases,
please contact Sterling Special Sales at 800-805-5489 or specialsales@sterlingpublishing.com.

Manufactured in the United States of America

4 6 8 10 9 7 5 3

www.sterlingpublishing.com

Dedication

To Victor Dorff, my wise and wonderful husband who makes books and life better, and to my dear siblings (in birth order): Maggie Sonne Dobbins, Chris Sonne, and James Sonne

Contents

Introduction

*T*here are gems of wisdom in this book that have survived thousands of years and helped millions of people of various faiths and doubts have happier, more peaceful, loving lives. More than 2,500 years ago, a man named Siddhartha Gautama meditated until he became a Buddha: the Enlightened and Awakened One. He then shared a plan for how anyone could overcome suffering in the world.

When you see statues of the Buddha, he often looks so serene, calm, and happy; sometimes there is a slight smile as if he knows something we want to know. What's the secret?

The Buddha did not mean to keep it a secret. He taught for almost five decades so others could continue the teachings through time with messages about how each of us has access to answers and happiness *in* us. He taught to rich and poor, male and female, educated and ignorant alike—at a time when teaching to women and the lower Hindu castes of untouchables was considered radical.

Long before modern science, he taught the mind-body connection that humans can develop to help recognize and control their thoughts, feelings, and behavior. He taught that everything alive in the world is interconnected and any one creature's actions can affect the others for harm or benefit. He taught that life is impermanent and ever changing; that we should live in the Now.

From his own experiences, he suggested The Middle Way. He had not found contentment in the luxurious, princely life of his first decades, nor did he find peace during his seven years exploring the various ascetic spiritual systems of his times, including self-mortification. Instead, he found the answers by meditating.

To find peace, kindness, wisdom, and a liberating path from suffering, he taught that we need to see how life *really* is, and then let go of the unneeded attachments—the greed, jealousy, hate, pride, anger, and regret that cause pain—and live mindfully with compassion. From the muddy muck of life, he promised, lotus flowers grow.

Buddha did not intend to be a deity or an institution, but over time in different parts of the world, the Buddha's teachings were adapted by people who adopted them, as they combined his lessons with other systems and needs. Now, there are a huge number of varieties of "Buddhism" as a religion, philosophy, form of government, and, in the West, a part of psychology.

His teachings spread through the centuries from India to the south (Thailand, Cambodia, Laos, Myanmar/Burma, and Sri Lanka). There, a branch of Buddhism called Theravada developed. The Buddha's teachings were orally transmitted, then later recorded in a phonetic version of the Buddha's language of Pali.

Disciples who disagreed with the Theravada interpretations of the Buddha's teachings developed Mahayana Buddhism that spread through India and other Himalayan nations, as well as north to China, Japan, Tibet, and Korea. Mahayana Buddhism intermingled with the older Taoism, Confucianism, and Shintoism philosophies. Mahayana texts and commentaries of the Buddha's teachings were written in Sanskrit.

Today, there is a dynamic evolution going on, as the Buddhist vehicles of meditation and mindfulness are being adapted in western secular and spiritual life. There are hundreds of Buddhist websites, apps, and podcasts. The American military, corporations like General Mills, Ivy League business schools, celebrities including Oprah and Richard

Gere, and major hospitals are incorporating aspects of Buddhist meditation and mindfulness into their own brands of well-being and health.

Parts of Buddhism once marginalized in the West or reserved for monasteries in the East are now mainstream.

The vitality and variety of Buddhism are thriving—from monks living secluded in caves to some of the most dynamic leaders for peaceful change who are active Buddhists.

Both Aung San Suu Kyi of Myanmar/Burma and His Holiness, the 14th Dalai Lama of Tibet have received Nobel Peace Prizes.

The Venerable Thich Nhat Hanh was nominated for the Peace Prize for his work in Vietnam and writes popular books about "engaged Buddhism," in which he describes how meditation and mindfulness can make the world better.

From the start, the Buddha was interested in practical ways to end the world's suffering, so people would be able to let go of the ignorance and illusion that caused them pain.

When some of his followers debated about theological issues and doctrine, the Buddha asked them a hypothetical question about a poisoned arrow. If you had a poisoned arrow in you, he asked, would you insist on knowing who made the arrow, what kind of tree the arrow was made of, or if the arrow's feathers were from a peacock? Would you let the poison take its horrible effect while you seek details about the stature and upbringing of the doctor who could pull the arrow out? Or would you want the arrow pulled out immediately so you could live and heal, be happy, and help others?

The Buddha offered ways to pull out our poison arrows, to make the lotus blossom, and to have a good and *great* life.

This book contains some golden pieces of the Buddha's wisdom. The pages in your hands include a blend of Buddhist principles, quotes, parables, meditational art exercises, and even a look at how your own breathing can help you relax. Real Buddhism is not in a book, though, but in the practice. Activating the vehicles of meditation and mindfulness with the Buddha's wisdom and discipline can help you see clearly and "let go" of your causes of discontent.

Like any aspect of life, if you focus on what this book does *not* have, you can be unhappy. It's not comprehensive, a quick fix, or a history. It is not scholarly, and it is not perfect. If you delve into what these pages *do* have, however, and combine it with what *you* have, you could change your life and the world for the better.

Or you could put it down and do something else. The Buddha urged that people not swallow any doctrine whole, but question every philosophy, test it out, and adapt it before adopting it. For the Buddha, it was not "my way or the highway," but rather, "here's a great way."

This book is a little well of wisdom, fed by an endless aquifer from the Buddha, cultivated through the ages by those who know far more than the author. Quench your thirst. Water your good seeds within. Share the ladle and the bucket with others. This book is small, but the Buddha's wisdom is infinite.

Maybe you will take one saying from this book that helps you be happier and kinder. Or perhaps the book will motivate you to meditate deeply, which will lead to unflappable, lasting joy. In any event, we hope you will personally enjoy the sublime "half smile" on the faces of so many Buddha statues meant to remind you that you too can be Awakened.

Part One

UNDERSTANDING
THE BUDDHA

Principles and Path

*A*fter the Buddha "woke up" from his intense meditation and decided to share his insights more than twenty-five centuries ago, he said all he really taught were "suffering and the end of suffering."

Over time, however, hundreds of thousands of pages have been written based on the forty-five years the Buddha spent teaching. Some of the most basic wisdom is summarized in enduring "to do" lists about how "to be": the Four Noble Truths, the Noble Eightfold Path, the Three Jewels, the Three Poisons, the Four Divine Abidings, and the Five Moral Precepts. Although any and all of these could add to your life, there is no instant Buddhism by the numbers.

The Buddha urged each person to keep an open heart and an open mind, and to explore ideas deeply before accepting or rejecting them. Meditation is one method of exploration. Another is to practice the principles taught by the Buddha and to pay attention to what happens.

Practicing the principles is more important than studying them. As the saying goes, "The arm that points to the moon is not the same as the moon." The following concepts will point toward finding enlightenment within, but they are not Enlightenment.

Buddhist sages have also pointed out that, while these teachings are the vehicles to get you to the other side of the river—from discontent to true Enlightenment—once you reach the other shore, you will no longer need those vehicles.

The Four Noble Truths

In the Buddhist view, the motivation of the Four Noble Truths is to make this life better for ourselves and others, and to reach Nirvana is to escape *samsara*, which is the word (in both Pali and Sanskrit) for the endless cycle of birth, death, and suffering.

1. Suffering is universal. "Suffering" is the translation usually used for the Pali word *dukkah* (or *duhkha* in Sanskrit), which can also mean discontent, stress, or thirst.

2. The cause of suffering is desire. "Desire" is the translation usually used for *tanah* in Pali (or *trishna* in Sanskrit), as in grasping at, lust after,

and craving for what we don't have, or holding on too tightly to what we do have.

3. The cure for suffering is the elimination, the "letting go," of desires and cravings.

4. The way to diminish or to let go of desire is to follow the Middle Way, to pursue the Noble Eightfold Path.

At first, this fundamental focus on suffering may seem negative, but the process is actually hopeful and practical. The Four Noble Truths not only point out the disease, but they offer a prescription for the cure. In this existence, if death and disease are accepted instead of feared, we can feel more joy and appreciate more "present moments" in life. Never take this minute—or any other—for granted.

Truth is freedom. We can be liberated—untethered from unhappiness—only if we avoid becoming entangled in needless want and clinging to old wounds, negative habits, wrong ideas, and unimportant things.

The Noble Eightfold Path

Although the Buddha taught that our emotions, illusions, and cravings shackle us to unhappiness, he also offered the Noble Eightfold Path as a way to liberation. All eight factors need to be achieved, but can be worked on simultaneously. They are often pictured as the eight spokes of a wheel, all working together. They support each other for a wise, disciplined, virtuous, and happy life that *is* the Middle Way to Enlightenment. Below are very short introductions to each of the factors and the categories to which they belong, but they all merit far more exploration to be understood best.

Wisdom, Insight, Understanding, Thought (*Panna* in Pali, *Pranja* in Sanskrit)

1. Right View, or Right Knowledge: Acknowledging what is, not denying it or altering it with wishful thinking or old habits; keeping the Four Noble Truths always in view.

2. Right Resolve, or Right Intention-Thinking: Keeping the thoughts and attitudes that further one's path; eliminating the obstructive attachments and thoughts.

Virtue, Ethical Conduct (*Sila* in both Pali and Sanskrit)

3. Right Speech: Speaking only when it will be useful, truthful, and not harmful to self or others.

4. Right Conduct, or Right Action: Acting with compassion and love, without causing harm to self or others.

5. Right Livelihood: Making a living in ways that are compatible with

right speech and right conduct; not lying, cheating, or making things that could kill, harm, or intoxicate other living creatures.

Mental Discipline, Cultivation, and Concentration (*Samhadhi* in both Pali and Sanskrit)

6. Right Effort: Being vigilant about eliminating unwanted qualities, habits, and thoughts, and about cultivating endeavors that support the Noble Eightfold Path.

7. Right Mindfulness: Being in the power of Now, aware fully of the present, not entangled in past or future.

8. Right Concentration: Staying focused, attentive on worthy subjects; *not* multitasking.

"Right," in this context, is not the opposite of wrong. Judgment is not part of the plan. Instead, "right" is the customary translation of the Sanskrit word *summa* (meaning perfect). Our word "summit" has a similar origin. You have reached the top if you can embody the below.

The Three Poisons

Most of the thoughts and actions that we should "let go" for the sake of our happiness and awakening are connected to what Buddhists call the

Three Poisons. This trio is what keeps us attached to the past and the future, instead of the moment we are in.

1. Greed: craving, possessiveness
2. Hatred: anger, aversion
3. Illusion: foolishness, ignorance, lies

The Three Jewels

The Three Jewels form the basic structure of Buddhism and are the great antidotes to the Three Poisons. Practitioners are said to "take refuge" in the Three Jewels.

1. Buddha: This refers both to the Supreme Buddha who awakened more than 2,500 years ago, and the Buddha nature in each of us—that is, the potential for each of us to awaken both to our wise, compassionate, nonharming, truth-seeking natures *and* to the understandings needed for ultimate Enlightenment to be a Buddha.

2. *Dhamma* (in Pali) or *Dharma* (in Sanskrit): These are the teachings of the Buddha, the truths and insights sought by those on the path to Enlightenment.

3. *Sangha* (in Pali) or *Samgha* (in Sanskrit): This is the community of monks and nuns who have kept the Buddha's teachings alive for

centuries. They comprise what is possibly the oldest continuing monastic practice.

This Jewel also refers to Buddhist communities formed to support the process and practice of seeking Enlightenment and awakening. For some branches of Buddhism, the Sangha has specific parameters; for others, the "community" could be loosely formed and flexible for anyone in the interconnected web practicing compassion and seeking wisdom.

At any moment, there are probably thousands of people in the world chanting this ancient Pali affirmation:

Buddham saranam gacchami.	I take refuge in the Buddha.
Dhammam saranam gacchami.	I take refuge in the Dhamma.
Sangham saranam gacchami.	I take refuge in the Sangha.

The Five (Moral) Precepts

The Five Precepts are at the core of Buddhist teachings. In today's language, some hesitate to call these precepts "moral," because that word can be loaded with judgment and a sense of superiority. They are meant to guide a life of virtue and concentration as a means to avoid suffering. Each of the factors in the Noble Eightfold Path can be applied to uphold the Five Precepts, and the Five Precepts can all counsel the path. Each of the precepts traditionally states what *not* to do, without dictating how to accomplish it. Because everything changes, the "how" may change, too.

1. "Do not kill" applies to all animals as well as humans. One should not intentionally kill or command others to kill or to harm any living creature. Further, one should try to protect living creatures and to show loving kindness to all interconnected life. When it comes to mealtime, some interpret this precept to dictate vegetarianism. Others believe the precept is being followed if they gratefully eat only those animals that have been humanely killed by others. The point is, we are all one, and harm to another is really harm to ourselves.

2. "Do not steal" applies to people's material things, as well as to time and to other intangible resources. Taken further, this precept encourages generosity. One should share one's abundance and give freely (money, material things, time, knowledge, and kindness) both to those in need and to those who have helped along the way, including parents, friends, and teachers.

3. "Do not indulge in sexual misconduct" includes the prohibition of specific hurtful acts like adultery and rape, but it also goes beyond that. Sexual desire is a major source of human craving and suffering, and this

precept calls for the avoidance of anything that causes physical or mental harm in our personal relations.

4. "Do not lie" proscribes outright lying, half-truths, exaggerations, gossip, and understatements. At a societal level, cultures function more peacefully and effectively when members exhibit a vigorous respect for the truth. At a deeper, personal level, respect for the truth is considered the key to liberation from suffering. The idea that happiness has to do with one's self or ego, with controlling external events, and with acquisition is a lie. Death and change are inevitable, and we are not "separate" from others. Realizing these truths is what will free us from illusion and suffering.

5. "Do not take intoxicants" applies to drugs, alcohol, cigarettes, and other things that can harm the body and affect the mind—specifically one's control of the mind. This is particularly important for people who meditate and practice mindfulness since the goal is to uncloud the mind, not alter the clarity of consciousness. Meditation and mindfulness are ways to let pollutants settle out. Intoxicants can shake and jiggle the negative debris back into the clarity. Taken further, this precept is also applied to protecting the living earth from toxins as well as people from the harm of intoxicants.

The Four Divine Abidings

Sometimes called the "Four Immeasurables" or Bhramavihara, the Divine Abidings provide immersive material for meditators to create divine places in their minds and hearts—for their own happiness and for others.

1. Loving Kindness (*Metta* in Pali, *Maitri* in Sanskrit): Loving kindness for others is a sincere genuine wish that everyone find well-being, contentedness, and happiness (regardless of their character and actions). Affection, approval, or friendship are not needed to feel loving kindness toward each and every person and creature.

2. Compassion (*Karuna* in both Pali and Sanskrit): Compassion is truly to want all humans to be released from suffering and its causes, without pity, judgment, or expectation of receiving anything in return.

3. Altruistic Joy (*Mudita* in both Pali and Sanskrit): Altruistic joy is gladness for others' gladness. Joy in the pleasure, happiness, and success of others—without jealousy, anger, competitiveness, or envy—can be a delightful bliss.

4. Equanimity (*Upekkha* in Pali; *Upeksa* in Sanskrit): Equanimity is a calm balance, without overindulgence or depravation and hurtful sacrifice. It involves seeing and accepting things as they are now, knowing that it all changes and that sometimes you can help make the change better,

but not attaching to negative emotions (like anger, regret, sadness) when you can't change things for the better. Sometimes referred to as the Middle Way, equanimity eschews ignorance, attachment, aversion, and indifference in favor of loving kindness, compassion, truth, and serenity.

Breathing

*B*reathing is an essential part of meditation, mindfulness, a Middle Way—and just plain life!

Regardless of your belief system, breathing is the heart (and lungs) of your earthly existence. We might live a few days without water, but without air, we die within minutes.

Take a moment to close your eyes and just pay attention to your normal breathing in and out.

When you focused on your breath, did you feel calmer? Most of us don't notice our breath until we are short of it—huffing up a hill, staying underwater a bit too long, or nursing a bad cold. Unless we are certain kinds of musicians or athletes or yoga fans, we may never have given much thought to how we breathe. It just seems to happen.

The average person takes a breath (that is, breathes in and out) about twenty times a minute when awake and sixteen to eighteen times a minute when sleeping. That adds up fast! Here are some estimates of every breath we take:

1,200 breaths an hour (awake)
27,000 breaths in 24 hours (a day and night sleeping 8 hours/night)
191,500 breaths in a week
10 million breaths in a year
780 million breaths in an average US life span (78 years)

Socrates admonished, "An unexamined life isn't worth living." What if you saw life as breath and just examined it for a while? People have been focusing on their breath in meditation for thousands of years.

There's a repeated tale about a monk who meditated on his breathing, day after day, as his teacher had instructed. He complained, "This is boring. Why is breathing so important?"

His teacher asked him to walk to the lake with him. At the shore's edge the student could see the lake reflecting the clouds and the sun, the light and the shadows, and he remembered about how meditation helped him to reflect. He also remembered that when thoughts distracted him, he was to treat them like a pebble that has disturbed the surface but can gently float to the bottom as the top becomes tranquil again.

His teacher told him to walk into the water with him, waist-high. Without warning, the teacher dunked the student underwater and held him there until he was wriggling mightily from lack of air.

Finally, the teacher released the student, who came up gasping. The teacher asked, "Now do you understand the importance of breathing?"

Breathing is the only system in our body that is both involuntary and voluntary. It happens unconsciously and we can consciously control its pace and volume, which can then affect our involuntary heart rate. Through breathing, we can actually switch over from our "fight or flight" sympathetic nervous system to our more relaxed parasympathetic nervous system.

No wonder people say, "Take a deep breath" when perceived stress, panic, or fear are nearby.

When your lungs, diaphragm, and thorax are helping you breathe, they are also acting as a pump for your heart and your lymph system, which helps combat sickness and disease.

Focusing on breath for our temporal well-being and health is an important level. In meditation, focus on breathing can also help us treat not just the symptoms, but also the causes of our suffering. Many people perseverate with unhealthy thoughts and worries, and hold onto old hurts. Breathing is the start of meditation, which can clear the mind of distractions, facilitating deep connections to changing consciousness.

The importance of breathing is revealed in the words we use to describe the process. In English, the word for breathing in (or inhaling) is *inspiration*. According to *Merriam-Webster's Dictionary*, the same word is also defined as "a divine influence or action on a person believed to qualify him or her to receive and communicate sacred revelation" and "the action or power of moving the intellect or emotions." The Online Etymology Dictionary traces the word back to the 1300s and the old French and late Latin words for "immediate influence of God or god."

The English word for breathing out (or exhaling), "expiration," also refers to "the fact of coming to an end or the point at which something ends," according to *Merriam-Webster*. More pointedly, to expire can mean to die.

The simple cycle of a single breath, in and out, followed by another inhalation and exhalation, reminds us of the cycles of birth and death, of the impermanence of all, of the value of the immediate Now, and of our interconnectedness. While breath connects our heart and body, it can also connect to something much greater.

As the chart below shows, the words used for "breath" in other languages contain similarly broader meanings.

Language	Word	Meanings
Latin	*spiritus*	soul, breath, courage
Greek	*pneuma*	spirit or a person, breath
Sanskrit	*prana*	life force, universal energy
Sanskrit	*atma*	breath, soul, essence
Chinese	*qior ch'l*	physical life force, breath

Interconnected Breath

The physical sciences teach us that all matter is recycled and is never lost. The tree that burns in a fire becomes the ashes that fertilize soil for other trees to grow. In that interconnected sense, what you are breathing may have been molecules that were once breathed by Cleopatra, Moses, Saladin, Benjamin Franklin, or a little old man from Pasadena. Or you may be breathing in molecules of air that once helped sustain the life of an elephant, dolphin, or dog. This is just another reminder of interconnectivity.

In some forms of Buddhism the focus on breath is to clean out all the other stuff in the mind. Other traditions believe you are breathing in the energy of the universe and can harness it. Full belly breathing is recommended to reach the spot below the navel believed to be the source of great energy.

Breathing (something we all have in common) is an ancient tool used to develop spiritual transformation. In his *Heart of the Buddha's Teaching*, Thich Nhat Hanh calls conscious breathing a joy: "When I discovered the Discourse on the Full Awareness of Breathing, I felt I was the happiest person on earth. These exercises have been transmitted by a community that has been practicing them for 2,600 years."

The Discourse he refers to is the sutra *Anapanasati*, which focuses on breath in meditation as a means to enlightenment. In it, the Buddha is quoted:

1. Breathing in a long breath, I know I am breathing in a long breath. Breathing out a long breath, I know I am breathing out a long breath.

2. Breathing in a short breath, I know I am breathing in a short breath. Breathing out a short breath, I know I am breathing out a short breath.

3. Breathing in, I am aware of my whole body. Breathing out, I am aware of my whole body.

4. Breathing in, I calm my whole body. Breathing out, I calm my whole body.

5. Breathing in, I feel joyful. Breathing out, I feel joyful.

6. Breathing in, I feel happy. Breathing out, I feel happy.

7. Breathing in, I am aware of my mental formations. Breathing out, I am aware of my mental formations.

8. Breathing in, I calm my mental formations. Breathing out, I calm my mental formations.

9. Breathing in, I am aware of my mind. Breathing out, I am aware of my mind.

10. Breathing in, I make my mind happy. Breathing out, I make my mind happy.

11. Breathing in, I concentrate my mind. Breathing out, I concentrate my mind.

12. Breathing in, I liberate my mind. Breathing out, I liberate my mind.

13. Breathing in, I observe the impermanent nature of all dharmas. Breathing out, I observe the impermanent nature of all dharmas.

14. Breathing in, I observe the disappearance of desire. Breathing out, I observe the disappearance of desire.

15. Breathing in, I observe the no-birth, no-death nature of all phenomena. Breathing out, I observe the no-birth, no-death nature of all phenomena.

16. Breathing in, I observe letting go. Breathing out, I observe letting go.

"The Full Awareness of Breathing, if developed and practiced continuously according to these instructions," the Buddha said, "will be rewarding and of great benefit."

The Sutra also says the Buddha asked that each specific breathing focus (numbers 3 through 16) be practiced. The results could be profound. Most of us, though, may need some warm-up sessions for a while to get to know our breathing better.

Many of us don't even know how we breathe. When some people concentrate on a deep breath in, they actually contract their stomach muscles as if that helps to pull more air to the lungs. If you are filling the cavities in your body naturally and fully with air while you inhale, your belly will rise as it fills with air. Witness a baby or the Buddha's belly.

Other ways to focus on your breath:

◄ Try closing your eyes (unless you are driving or performing surgery). We receive an enormous amount of information through our eyes, and it can distract us. Now, with your eyes closed, focus on your breath.

◄ The nose knows. Focus and feel the air going in and out of your nostrils. Is the air going out warmer than the air coming in? Are both your nostrils clear? Does your breath alternate nostrils?

◄ Some practitioners focus on their abdomen. It may even help you at first to put your hands on your belly to feel the differences of inhales and exhales.

◄ Mentally counting can help you concentrate. "One" with air going in, and "one" with it going out. Then two. Then three. See if you can get to five or ten without your attention straying. If it does, gently begin the count again.

◄ Follow the path of air in your normal breathing. Then breathe deeply or more slowly, and see what muscles and body parts feel the difference in the act and the effects.

For Buddhist meditations, most observation of breathing is to note the natural rhythms, which will slow and deepen, or to time the breath with certain mental thoughts or vocal chants. The goal is to use breath to go beyond the symptoms of problems (our mental chatter based often on the Three Poisons or the Five Precepts) and continue on the path to Enlightenment.

Meditation

*H*ave you always wanted to be a wild animal tamer? Or control minds? Welcome to meditation. The animal you can tame is you, and the mind you can control is your own.

We want more control in our lives, and we often act as if it's all about controlling the people and things around us. Too often we focus on the others we want to direct and to affect what they decide, think of us, vote, buy, and do.

Imagine if instead we practiced to know, to develop, and to control our *own* minds—to recognize, and let go of, chatter about petty worries, problems that haven't happened yet, gossip, re-played hurts, plots for revenge or gain, yearning for things we don't have. Imagine just feeling in love with being part of the whole glorious splendor of life.

Imagine if we could discern our own emotional patterns and ways of thinking, recognize the negative habits and impulses, and say good-bye to them in a way that didn't cause harm. Imagine if loving kindness replaced gossip, and joy replaced judgment. For centuries, Buddhists have used meditation as the transformative way to replace the unwholesome with the wholesome.

Sometimes our day's emotions and thoughts fill us with anger, worries, self-doubts, and other half-chewed garbage. We may think we are "letting go" of all that when we reach for a drink or turn on the television, but the next day those negative feelings will still be there.

Meditation can help us "let go" of those unneeded thoughts.

The value of meditation is sometimes described by a gardening analogy: Meditating can help plant and cultivate the good seeds. It probably won't kill the bad seeds (desire, greed, jealousy, anger, regret...). They continue to exist, but they may stay dormant, and not do harm, if not watered and fed with negative thoughts. If we pull out the weeds by their roots, we can better see the flowers and give them more room to grow.

Prepare to Meditate

It's been repeatedly said that meditation is simple, but it's not easy. In its most basic form, the instructions are, "Sit still, and still your mind." But whether you actually sit or lie down or walk, and whether your mind is stilled through techniques of breathing, chanting, visualization, concentrating on a single thing, or emptying out completely, the very stillness will be calming and beneficial.

With a still mind, as on the tranquil surface of an unperturbed lake or a clean mirror, reflections will appear that were not visible before. Birds and clouds will come and go. You may see yourself more clearly. And over time, you may learn to tame your inner animal and manage your mind.

Meditation can be a map, a mirror, or a spam filter. Like a "time-out" for a kid, or a "re-boot" for a computer, meditation can help us reset our well-being. If we are not spending our energies running away from things, or running toward things, but stay still, things can come to us—from within us.

For Buddhists through the ages, three factors of the Noble Eightfold Path (effort, mindfulness, and concentration) have been developed through meditation for better lives and for progress on the path to the final Enlightenment.

Even if we are not committed to Buddhism, however, our physiological and neural patterns change when we meditate. We relax. Just minutes a day of meditative breathing can be a free tonic for stress, anxiety, depression, fatigue, and confusion.

Psychologists and neurologists are currently gathering evidence of what the Buddha knew twenty-five centuries ago—meditation can help us better manage our thoughts and emotions.

Begin

The best way to start is, simply, to start. Pick a time, and give it a try—not just once, but repeatedly. Experiment. Be open-minded and openhearted. There are walking meditations, laying down meditations, standing meditations, and many schools of meditation. The section on mindfulness will share some activities that can be meditative, and the chapter on art will share creative meditations, but for starters, you might want to take a seat.

Here is one basic template to get you started with seated meditation:

Place: Find a place you can feel safe and relaxed and are unlikely to be interrupted. This may be a corner in your home, or somewhere in a garden or park, or you may choose to join others in a meditational session. The Supreme Buddha meditated under a tree.

Position: Find a comfortable sitting position, with your upper torso tall and your shoulders back—ears, shoulders, and hips in alignment—so breathing can best nurture you. A cushion under the buttocks can help some. For others, a chair may be a better option. Sitting cross-legged with the foot of each leg on the thigh of the other is called the lotus position, and it is not comfortable for everyone. Some people sit "half lotus," with one of their feet on the other thigh. Others prefer to fold their knees, facing forward, and have their buttocks on their heels.

Hands: The position of the hands, called *mudras,* can be symbolic, as seen in statues of the Buddha. Trying one of those positions can be a way to try to connect to that ideal.

A classic "meditation mudra" is formed by laying one hand in the other, with both palms facing up and the tips of the thumbs touching just above the palms. The oval formed by the hands and thumbs represents a calming, cleansing energy.

The "mudra of understanding" is formed by touching the tip of the index finger to the tip of the thumb, as if holding a "grain of truth." The other three fingers are extended. This gesture symbolizes spiritual understanding.

The "mudra of supreme enlightenment" is formed by bringing the hands together at chest-level, with the index fingers touching and extended upward, while the other fingers are all intertwined. This gesture is also sometimes called the "best-perfection mudra."

Or, you may just want to rest your hands on your knees.

Now What?

Most beginners, and even some people who have been meditating for years, find it difficult just to clear their minds and sit peacefully, without lots of mental chatter. Here are some methods to develop your meditation session.

Breathing: Focus on the breath going in and out. When a thought distracts you, recognize it, but go back to focusing on the breath. (More details about the breath as a focal point of concentration during meditation can be found in the section on breathing on page 27.)

Chanting: For some, chanting is a way to fill the consciousness with positive thoughts so there is no room for painful or harmful thoughts. Chanting can also be a way to develop the attributes chanted. A *mantra* is a phrase that is repeated rhythmically, in conjunction with the breath. Some students are assigned a mantra by a teacher, and it may be in Sanskrit. Others make up their own phrases to repeat during the breath in and another for the breath out.

"Om mani padme hum," which can be roughly translated as, "The Jewel is in the lotus," is a famous and popular chant. It is considered to be the mantra of the bodhisattva (one whose essence is enlightenment) of compassion.

Some chant the name of the Buddha, with the belief that the sound creates a vibrational energy that can purify or protect. One sect of Buddhism, known as the Pure Land Buddhists, believe that by focusing all their attention on repeating the name of Amitabha Buddha, they are assured rebirth in a promised land without distractions, where the presence of Buddhas and other Enlightened Ones will make it easier to achieve enlightenment.

Subjects: Some forms of meditation encourage meditators to empty their minds. This does not mean to space out or fall asleep. On the contrary, it means to vigilantly keep the mind in a receptive state. The metaphor used to support the value of emptying the mind for meditation is that one cannot pour tea into a full teacup. Only when the teacup of the mind is empty is there room for new knowledge.

Meditating on any one object—a fly or bookshelf—may lead to insights about how interconnected everything is. The bookshelf may be made of wood that came from a tree that needed light from the sun and rain and soil, and a person to make the bookshelf—a person who had a mother and father and children—and the bookshelf may have been transported across an ocean on a ship, a ship made of metal that was mined by . . . whom? More meditation could also ponder the causes and effects that lead each person and part of nature to be at the particular juncture to help make the bookshelf. It can be endless.

Key Buddhist teachings could also provide matter for meditation, or you may want to use something that appears to you during your *own* meditation. Instead of gently pushing it aside, you can take one of your thoughts and try to figure out why it is part of your being.

Patience: Quieting the mind is only the first step in meditation. In losing our sense of self through meditation, we may gain an opportunity to find our *true* self. In meditation, we can sometimes be outside of time and body and feel connected to a great Oneness that comes with a beautiful sense of love and happiness. We may have glimpses of the interdependence and connectivity of everything. For a moment, we may even grasp that the duality of "us" and "them"—of an "I" separate from everything else—is merely an illusion. Everything we do matters—to everyone and to everything. We may feel great calm or joy or wisdom, with deep flashes of understanding.

Then, there are also the times when the jumping, niggling, flea-thoughts in our brains just keep biting and won't fly away. We may feel like we are in a snowstorm of emotions with little inner visibility. The right knee hurts. The left ear itches. You are twitching to get up and move.

When any of that happens, and you find you are just plain irritated, try letting a half-smile grace your face like the Buddha and be amused that you are in fact human. Return your focus to your breath and to the moment . . . then, to the next breath and the next moment. The distractions may disappear. Or new ones may come. Either way, it is part of the process.

Learning to tame our wild animal and control our mind takes time, patience, persistence, and loving kindness toward ourselves. Not every meditation is going to be all comfy and fun. It can be relaxing, restorative, revealing. It's an ongoing process. It can make your life better, and therefore others' lives better, too.

Committing to meditating every day, even if for only ten minutes, could help you physically, emotionally, and mentally and be the catalyst for much deeper spiritual contentment over time. Longer, more refined meditation can truly yield profound insights, and changes in outlook, behavior, and results in life. But for starters—start. Say "hello" to the Buddha nature in you—the best of you—and listen.

Mindfulness

*M*indfulness is being aware and attentive of what is going on at this very moment, the Now. Mindfulness is being "awake" in the moments of our life. It is a key aspect of meditation, as well as a useful means for anyone to interact better with his or her daily life.

The path of the Middle Way isn't in yesterday or tomorrow. It exists *right now*.

Being in the presence of Now is a way to stop clinging to the past of hurts, grudges, and regrets; to the future of wants and cravings; and to all the other distractions in our lives. Those distractions are the illusions that keep us from seeing things as they really are, from being truly present in our lives, from being aware of the gifts of the present, of Now.

In the modern world today, we seem to live in a realm aimed at distracting us from Now. We experience far more external sensory bombardment than any other creatures in the history of the world. Yet, we work on adding more channels, more apps, more tunes, more passport stamps, more virtual friends, and more appointments to our lives, even as we complain that we don't have enough time for those we have already collected.

Our culture and economy are based on consumerism—on wanting to possess what we don't already have. The Buddhist idea of mindfulness is being aware of what you already have, both externally and internally.

Stop. Right now.

Look around you.

Smell, feel, hear, taste, touch, and engage your mind in this moment. This moment will never be again. If you miss it, it is gone. When your mind starts to pass judgment or to jump around like a monkey to distract you with other things, focus on your breath. Engage your senses. Be aware of where and when you are. Right now.

"Live in the now" is not the same as "Indulge! Do whatever you want, for tomorrow we may die." The latter choice is ignorance and can cause interconnected harm to you, to others, and to the world. Instead, "being in the now" means being aware, and making everything you do, even the most mundane tasks, make a difference in the web of cause and effect. In practice, being in the Now, mindfully, will make you less selfish and more selfless, with greater happiness.

The Great Buddha taught that an unmindful person who indulges in selfish instant gratification is like a child licking honey from a sharp knife. The child will be hurt, and ultimately so will others. Being mindful, can mean being aware of a craving for honey, and observant of the consequences of the knife. That mindfulness helps us make better choices.

In Buddhism, mindfulness is one of the key factors on the Noble Eightfold Path, a main part of meditations, and a tool to help us in our daily intentions, thoughts, and actions away from the harm of the Three Poisons (greed, illusion, and hate) and toward the happiness of the Four Divine Abidings (loving kindness, compassion, altruistic joy, and equanimity). Mindfulness can help us live fully The Five Precepts (no lying, no stealing, no killing, no sexual misconduct, and no intoxicants), and instead perform kindnesses toward ourselves, other people, and all living things.

Thich Nhat Hanh, in *Living Buddha, Living Christ*, repeats a story that exemplifies how mindfulness can be a part of every aspect of life:

"When the Buddha was asked, 'Sir, what do you and your monks practice?' he replied, 'We sit, we walk, and we eat.' The questioner continued, 'But sir, everyone sits, walks, and eats,' and the Buddha told him, 'When we sit, we know we are sitting. When we walk, we know we are walking. When we eat, we know we are eating.'"

Hanh continues writing that mindfulness can be a healing agent for ourselves and others: "When we are mindful, touching deeply the present moment, we can see and listen deeply, and the fruits are always understanding, acceptance, love, and the desire to relieve suffering and bring joy."

The long-practiced mindfulness of Buddhism is now being integrated into mainstream secular western life as a tool that can unify mind and body to ease a range of ailments, from lack of concentration—a crippling factor in the workplace and in education—to the kind of stress that can be harmful to our immune system and happiness. After studying Buddhism, Dr. Jon-Kabat-Zinn founded MBSR (Mindfulness-Based Stress Reduction), which is used by hundreds of medical programs to help people change habits and put them on the path to better health.

Dr. Daniel Goleman's bridging of philosophies and psychologies of East and West have touched countless lives through a book on meditation published in 1977 (*The Meditative Mind: The Varieties of Meditative Experience*), to his best seller *Emotional Intelligence* (1995), and his continuing current work to share mindfulness from the lamas to the laboratories and living rooms.

On his website, His Holiness the 14th Dalai Lama of Tibet also urges that science continue to study how Buddhist techniques work in order to help all kinds of people process negative emotions and behavior: "We need to combine our material development with the inner development of such human values as compassion, tolerance, forgiveness, contentment, and self-discipline."

Being aware in the Now, is a liberating vehicle that allows our consciousness to grow—whether for samsara escape from the Wheel of Life and Death or to stop the daily suffering we needlessly create.

How much of your thinking revolves around "if only . . ."? Some of us have regrets about the past, as in, "If only I had . . ." Others daydream about conditions for the future that we think will somehow provide happiness, such as, "If only I owned a…"

"If" is conditional. It's not real! Try dwelling in what *is*, right now.

Mindful Exercises

It's lovely in meditation to sit quietly, to breathe deeply, to be mindful, and to feel an inner peace. But when you get up and head out, if you revert to old patterns quickly—screaming at the contractor on the phone or cursing the traffic when you drive—then your Buddha nature is not being fully tapped. Mindfulness can make ordinary life more extraordinary, and, for most westerners, there are exercises that can help to develop mindfulness as a way of being—as a more steady state.

Listen: Try for one hour not to multitrack or multitask or multi-ask. Just do one thing well. Really *listen*—with your heart and with your mind—to whomever you are with. Don't judge, try to control, or analyze. Just *listen*—with compassion and love. Even if—or maybe *especially if*—the person you are with is just you, listen well.

This doesn't sound difficult, but some people cannot do it for more than a few minutes. Don't give up because it didn't seem natural or easy at first.

Pick an activity you love—gardening, driving, golf, eating. Whatever it is, there are ways to do it mindfully. Start by slowing down and really paying attention. Discipline yourself so your thoughts don't wander. Try that activity with mindfulness for fifteen minutes, then lengthen the periods.

Similarly, take an activity you *don't* enjoy—some part of your work or a necessary chore—and try doing it mindfully. Be alert and focus on every aspect of the task. You may find it more fulfilling.

See how many daily activities you can do mindfully—brush your teeth, send an email. Engage your five traditional senses, and what some Buddhists consider the sixth sense: your mind.

To integrate mindfulness in your daily life beyond meditation, experts suggest that it may help if you give yourself reminders—on your daily calendar, a sound on your cell phone, a computer alert, or taped notes on your mirror and refrigerator. Let the reminder inspire mindfulness. You may want to post images of the Buddha or people who represent other qualities and ideals you desire, to remind yourself to be mindful. Or you may want to associate outward cues as catalysts—the postal carrier delivering the mail, the sun setting, sitting at a red light, or turning on a water faucet or a light— to bring your mind back to the full present and to be mindfully in Now.

In the Parables section of this book, "Carrying" and "Good? Bad?" demonstrate the value of mindfulness as a way to unite our inner and outer worlds, to let go of emotional baggage and judgment. In being mindful in your daily life, you may create your own parables to learn from.

In the next section, there are some ideas on how to incorporate mindfulness and meditation in the *art* of life.

Art and Buddhism

*T*he art forms of Buddhism range from those that have endured the millennia (architectural temples and *stupas*, statues of the Buddha, cave paintings, and painted scrolls called *thanghas*) to those that are deliberately impermanent, such as circular mandalas that are carefully, elaborately made with colored sands to show the cosmic understanding of the universe, then blown away, confirming that nothing lasts and everything changes. Buddhist art forms also range from the wildly complex designs of Tantric art to the Zen simplicity of a single brushstroke on tissue paper or carefully placed rocks in raked sand.

In large part, Buddhist art forms are related to meditation and mindfulness, and to the process of seeking relief from suffering.

In some areas of the world, Buddhist art may not even be regarded as "art" by the practitioners, who consider it a functional part of their daily lives. For example, in the Buddhist Himalayan Royal Kingdom of Bhutan, known for introducing the measurement of Gross National Happiness instead of Gross National Product, there are visually beautiful prayer wheels at temples and road intersections. Buddhists and visitors alike chant as they turn the wheels of prayers filled with paper scrolls for blessings for all.

People can also carry and spin personal prayer wheels. There are even prayer wheels artfully housed at the bases of most waterfalls, where the power of the water turns the wheels, continually sending prayers out to the trees, to the winds, and all sentient beings, whether or not humans are present.

Many of the Buddhist art forms that have most captured the curiosity of western culture were developed from Japanese Zen Buddhism, which evolved from the Chinese *Chan*. Though it may take years of training to master the true forms, the act of creation itself is spontaneous, like awakening. The processes require mindfulness and can be forms of meditation for the creator and the observer/participant. Examples of Zen arts include the tea ceremony, flower arranging, rock gardens, brush painting, and haiku. Each can take years to master, yet each could be introduced in a modified way to give beginners a sense of the peace and beauty involved in the process and the finished product.

Tea Ceremony

Buddhist monks are credited with bringing tea with them from China, many centuries after the Chinese began cultivating tea. One story says that the tea ceremony developed in Japan as a way to help monks lengthen their periods of meditation without falling asleep. Another says the tea ceremony developed in Japan because each meeting with others will never be repeated, and should be honored. Today, the traditional tea ceremony can be an exacting ritual of preparation and celebration in which the sip of tea alone can spark epiphany.

Tea ceremonies also have evolved with a rich practice outside of Buddhism and are considered an art form by many. The rituals and materials used in the ceremonies can vary, depending on the season, the time of day, and the purpose of the occasion. In some ceremonies, certain motions were prescribed by the sleeve lengths of kimonos, and remain that way even with western dress. A formal tearoom usually has calligraphy (often of a Buddhist message) and a flower arrangement.

For your own experiment in mindfulness, try sipping an entire cup of tea tranquilly in silence with all of you focused only on the moments. Fully experience the taste, smell, touch, sound, sight, and thought of the tea and your sipping. Practice body-awareness as the tea moves through your mouth, and as your arms and hands reach for the teacup again.

Try doing this exercise with someone else. Imagine you are that person, and focus on their sensations as yours. Try it again while drinking a cup of tea and imagining you are the tea.

Ikebana Floral Arrangement

The delicate precision of beautiful balance in flower arrangements with a true "in the moment" focus is traditionally done in silence. As in the Buddha's Middle Way, balance is all. Ikebana uses stems, berries, and leaves, as well as flowers. Shapes, forms, textures, and empty spaces created between colors and the vessel are all part of a lovely design. Traditional ikebana are designed only to be viewed from the front.

Some people think flower arranging traveled to Japan in the sixth century with Buddhist priests, as offerings on an altar to honor the Buddha and Buddha spirit, then later may have been used as ritual respect to the dead. The early teachers of ikebana were all Buddhists.

Through the centuries, ikebana became popular in secular Japan throughout all levels of society, and several thousand types of ikebana may have evolved.

Though traditional ikebana is very exacting with specific rules, "free-style" approaches have also become popular in modern times. For people anywhere, any flower arranging done mindfully can be beneficial.

Flower arrangement can be a meditative way to connect to the beauty of nature as well as to help reveal how one's own nature is connected to the greater natural world. A playful exercise for westerners would be to incorporate other parts of the flowers, and to stay quiet and mindful while arranging it all. Then sit quietly and look, without judgment, for symbolism that reveals nature in the arrangement.

Rock Gardens

Sometimes referred to as Zen gardens, the Japanese rock gardens are dry landscapes that represent nature. They are usually found at a temple, next to where the abbot of the monastery lives. Built in the foreground of a wall, Zen gardens provide a place for monks to meditate. To outsiders it may look like a sparse emptiness with some raked sand and rocks. They wouldn't be wrong.

Making the garden, maintaining the garden, and sitting and absorbing the garden are all forms of meditation for harmony. If the observer looks more knowingly, the raked sand can represent symbolic water (the ocean of mind, or the dharma river that needs crossing). The rocks may represent mountains or islands. The gardens are sometimes arranged as re-creations of mythical place or symbolic of the greater universe outside the garden or inside the meditator.

For those who can travel, visiting Zen gardens that are centuries old in Japan is profound. Sitting silently for a prolonged peaceful time on the platform above the quintessential Zen Garden of Ryoan-Ji in Kyoto, built in the fifteenth century, has changed modern people's lives.

Closer to home or office, many major US cities have Zen gardens. Some westerners make their own miniature rock gardens or find a corner in the yard to create a place for outdoor meditation. Try sitting al fresco for fifteen minutes, communing without pretext. Perhaps your mind will empty out a bit, too. An empty mind has room for revelation.

Brush-Stroke Painting, or Zenga

Zen brush-stroke painting and calligraphy, a rich tradition in Japan, can be another path or practice for "letting go" of the mental chatter that ties you to time frames other than Now. Art can absorb your attention away from the frazzling fragments of thought. You are present.

In *Zenga*, (a school of brush stroke and calligraphy) the Japanese have a form called *enso*, which translates as circle. A key symbol in Zen Buddhism, it can represent Enlightenment, as well as the void.

Being able to draw a true circle in one or two brushstrokes can demonstrate a clear mind-body connection. Some believe that what your circle looks like can tell much about who you are.

Monks might spend years to master an enso with brush strokes on silk or rice paper, which will blot if there is hesitation. Years of discipline focus on a moment. In the same manner they create calligraphy with black ink, monks train diligently with the thickness and thinness of lines, as well as the use of empty space.

Fortunately, the age you begin your practice is irrelevant. Kojima Kendo, an extraordinary Buddhist nun who set up an orphanage after World War II, didn't take up Zenga until she was 92 and broke her hip. She was still creating beautiful, balanced images at the age of 97.

Few people outside of monastic life have time for this kind of mastery, but there are still ways to benefit.

Buddha Board

A modern version of brush painting that is gaining popularity in our fast-paced world can be enjoyed on something called the Buddha Board.

The Buddha Board can be laid flat or set up on an easel to allow gravity to play a role with the levity of art. Using a brush or fingers dipped in water, strokes are made directly on the slate as kind of peaceful meditation.

Even as the artist begins to contemplate the blacks, whites, and grays of the images created on the board, the drawing begins to disappear as the water evaporates. Soon, the physical slate is blank and ready again for whatever comes next. Perhaps the artist, too, has a cleaner, clearer mental slate, or maybe a revelation arises from what came and went.

The impermanence of the image is a reminder of life's impermanence. All the scenes of our lives—whether fantastic, horrific, embarrassing, or sweet—come and go. If we try to cling to the moments when they are gone, we will suffer. If we spend too much time thinking about what we *want* to paint in our life, we will suffer. The alternative is to give full attention to painting now—or to accept the blank slate.

We see how absorbed kids are when they draw. This kind of presence and oneness when we forget about self and external things can be peaceful and joyful.

Some of the Zen-like challenges of the board:

◄ Pick a time when you won't be interrupted or distracted. Start without fear or expectation.

◄ Don't "think" while you are painting. Let go of thoughts about anything else. Try to be one with the art.

◄ Don't "attach" to the outcome of the results on the board with judgment, comparison, pride, regret, or ego.

◄ Observe your Buddha nature. What did you reveal about yourself? Did this spontaneous act from your unconscious make you more aware of your true nature? Were you happy forgetting about past and future worries?

◄ The impermanence of the image also challenges the human desire to possess. The idea, instead, is to "live in the moment"—to attend fully to the act and to enjoy it!

Haiku

Haiku is another ancient Buddhist art accessible to all—from gurus to schoolchildren to you.

Haiku is Now poetry, which uses a few words to describe a moment that could express or inspire some enlightenment.

Here are some haiku guidelines to help, not to restrict:

◄ In English, haiku poems are traditionally three lines with a 5-7-5 pattern of sounds or syllables, but the rules of the genre are subject to change. At one time, for example, the objective of haiku was to write a poem that could be easily read in one breath.

◄ The past and future are usually not mentioned.

◄ Adjectives are generally not used, because they imply an "I" and ego subjectivity.

◄ Nature is usually the focus.

◄ There is usually a reference to the season (the Now in the cycles of passing time), either directly (winter, fall) or indirectly, with the mention of a fruit, flower, weather, or activity of nature that is season specific.

◄ In top haiku, two phenomena are juxtaposed.

The Haiku Society of America was established in 1968, and its website has links to large online collections of haiku in English. Western haiku writers include literary stars like Jack Kerouac and Richard Wright. It's also taught in many schools to young children, who seem to grasp its immediacy. Now what about you?

For inspiration, try a Japanese *ginko*, or haiku walk—a stroll in nature to observe and to be attuned, culminating in the writing of poetry.

The Japanese sometimes go on ginkos with a group leader on specific occasions, like a solstice or when blossoms first appear. Walkers can bring a paper or electronic writing tablet and take notes or make drawings to prompt haiku later, or they may be inspired to write haiku on the walk.

If you're too comfortable to move, here are sample haikus to inspire you from four Japanese masters of the art:

An old silent pond.
A frog jumps into the pond.
Splash! Silence again.
—*Matsuo Basho (1644–1694)*

Flies swarm all over.
Whatever do they want with
These old wrinkled hands?
—*Kobyashi Issa (1763–1828)*

A cold winter blast.
The cord of a paddy hat
cut into my neck.

—Masaoka Shiki (1867–1902)

An evening cloudburst.
And sparrows cling desperately
To trembling bushes.

—Yosa Buson (1716–1783)

Parables

*L*ike other great spiritual leaders after him, the Buddha and his followers through the centuries used parables to teach and to prompt. Some of the following parables have been widely quoted, modified, and used by multiple faiths. They are often referred to as Buddhist because of the gist of their tales. They are offered here as pieces of the great peace.

The Buddha recommended that people accept knowledge based not on its external source, but on their own internal examination. Any one of these tales may prompt you to know your true self better. Or not.

Carrying and Letting Go

Two monks must cross a great river to reach the village on an errand for a monastery. When they approach the river, a woman is struggling to cross. One of the monks swiftly picks her up, carries her across the river, and places her on the other shore, where they part ways.

The second monk follows behind, keeping his distance, disturbed. For these monks, even being in the presence of a woman is forbidden.

After several miles, the second agitated monk bursts forth to his companion, "How could you do such a thing? How could you touch that woman?"

Replied the first monk, "I put that woman down miles ago. Why are you still carrying her?"

Good? Bad? Maybe.

There once was a farmer whose horse galloped away. His concerned neighbor clucked his tongue, "Poor you, what bad luck!" The farmer calmly replied, "Who knows if it is bad or good?"

A whole herd of horses appeared the next day, with the farmer's horse in the lead. The neighbor beamed, "Oh, how good! Congratulations!" The farmer calmly said, "Who knows if it is good or bad?"

The next week, the son of the farmer broke his leg terribly while riding one of the new horses. "Oh, dear, bad luck now," the neighbor shook his head. The farmer responded, "Who knows what is good and what is bad?"

Then the army came through, forcing young men to enlist. When they saw the boy's broken leg they left him on the farm, and marched on to war. The neighbor was back with more congratulations about the good news.

The sage farmer said, "Who knows what is good or what is bad?"

The Useful Pot

An elderly Chinese woman had two large pots, each hung on the opposite ends of a pole, which she carried across her neck. One of the pots was perfect and always delivered a full portion of water. The other pot had a visible crack in it and at the end of the long walk from the stream to the house, the cracked pot arrived only half full of water.

Every day, for a full two years, the woman brought home only one and a half pots of water. Of course, the perfect pot was proud of its accomplishments. But the cracked pot was ashamed of its own flaw, and unhappy that it could only do half of what it had been made to do.

After two years of what it perceived to be bitter ongoing failure, the cracked pot spoke to the woman one day by the stream. "I am ashamed of myself, because this crack in my side causes water to leak out all the way back to your house."

The old woman smiled, "Did you notice that there are lovely flowers on your side of the path, but there are no flowers on the other pot's side?

"That's because I have always known about your flaw. I planted flower seeds on your side of the path, and every day while we walk back, you water them. For two years, I have been able to pick these beautiful flowers to decorate the table. Without your being just the way you are, there would not be this beauty to grace the road and the house."

Heaven and Hell

A visitor to hell saw many people seated at a table on which many delicious foods were laid. Chopsticks more than a meter long were tied to their right hands, and their left hands were tied to their chairs.

Although the occupants of hell were able to reach the food with the chopsticks, their arms were too short to bring the food at the end of the long chopsticks into their mouths. They grew impatient and got their hands and chopsticks tangled with one another's. The delicacies were scattered here and there.

When the visitor arrived in heaven, he found much the same situation, with people sitting at a well-stocked table, extra-long chopsticks affixed to one free hand. The people of heaven, however, happily used the long chopsticks to pick out someone else's favorite food and feed it to him or her, and in turn they were being fed by others. They all enjoyed their meal in harmony.

Mustard Seed

A woman came to the Buddha, lamenting the death of her child and imploring him to restore her family. He tells her he will bring her child back to life if she can bring him a mustard seed from a house that has not known death.

The woman travels around the countryside, from home to home, in search of the prized mustard seed. Instead, she finds family after family with stories of death to share. A widow mourns the death of her husband of fifty years. A young man grieves over the recent loss of his parents. A retired soldier regales her with stories of his former comrades in arms.

Finally, she returns without the mustard seed, but with a better understanding of the first tenet of Buddhism: Suffering is a fact of life.

Wiser for her journey, the woman also found herself connected to all those who, like her, had lost loved ones.

The Buddha Within

The abbot of a once famous Buddhist monastery was deeply troubled that the monastery had seriously declined. Monks were lax in their practice, novices were leaving, and lay supporters were deserting to other centers.

The distraught leader traveled far to a sage and recounted his tale of woe. He explained how the monastery had once flourished and wondered how it could be revived to days of yore.

The sage looked him in the eye and said, "The reason your monastery has languished is that the Buddha is living among you in disguise, and you have not honored Him."

The abbot hurried back, his mind in turmoil.

The Selfless One was at his monastery! Who could He be? Brother Hua? . . . No, he was full of sloth. Brother Po? . . . No, he was too dull. But then, the Worthy One was in disguise. What better disguise than sloth or dull-wittedness?

The abbot called his monks to him and revealed the sage's words. They, too, were taken aback and looked at each other with suspicion and awe.

Which one of them was the Chosen One?

The disguise was perfect. Not knowing who He was, they took to treating everyone with the respect due to a Buddha. Their faces started shining with an inner radiance that attracted novices and then lay supporters.

In no time at all, the monastery far surpassed its previous glory.

Finding Your Way

*T*here is a Buddha nature in each of us. Meditation and mindfulness have been helping people find the best within for more than twenty-five centuries. They do not require external things or spending money. They do need internal commitment and spending time. Even a few minutes a day contemplating and practicing the wisdom of Buddha's teachings can help you find your best path.

The Buddha did not say, "*I* am the way." He said, "There *is* a way, and we must find it within ourselves." We must let go of our hurts and the hindrances that hamper us from enjoying the moments and letting our lives count.

From his own experiences, the Buddha offered the Middle Way between extremes, and the Noble Eightfold Path for happier, more meaningful passage. He shared the light of truth to see our way, and the vehicles of meditation and mindfulness. But he did not tell us there was only one correct journey for a happy, helpful life. He did not say you must follow him or be a Buddhist.

We can seek sangha-communities, practices, and environments that support us, but it is still the self (as understood in western upbringing) that needs to become selfless to be happier.

We can read more literature about the Dharma and continue to explore the Buddha intellectually, but it is the practice of compassion, loving-kindness, truth, and living in the mindful Now that will diminish our suffering and stop us from causing suffering to others.

Part Two of this book is a selection of Buddhist wisdom and advice, collected by various people, from the ancient Dhammapada beloved in Buddhist literature, and from more modern Buddhists: revered figures of the past, evolved leaders in Buddhism today, and western contemporaries who practice Buddhism.

Many great and eminently quotable Buddhists have not been included here. Presumably, they don't care, since ego should not be involved in living or in teaching the Dharma.

It is up to you how you want to merge Part One and Part Two with the best of you—your Buddha nature—how you want to mix wise sayings with principles, parables, and the practices of meditation, art, and mindfulness as you continue on your path.

You may choose to read a few pages a day, sip a cup of tea, write in the margins, pick up a paint brush, take a quote for a walk, sit with a saying, listen well, help a child, let go of some poisons, or breath mindfully.

You may try meditating every day for a month and beyond, commit to changing your character, let go of your garbage, help others, find your Buddha nature, and be joyful every morning you wake up on a path to an even greater awakening.

Whatever you choose, may the following help you find your way!

The time is now.

Part Two

WISDOM OF
THE BUDDHA

Select Verses from
Dhammapada: The Teachings of Buddha
Edited by Friedrich Max Muller

The Dhammapada is one of the most beloved and accessible masterpieces from early Buddhist texts. The anthology shares more than 400 verses of what the Buddha taught in many different settings and circumstances to spur good conduct, release from suffering, and spiritual growth. The verses were transmitted orally for centuries and later recorded many years after the Buddha's death in his spoken language: Pali. Dhamma (Dharma is Sanskrit) can be translated to mean teachings, truths, phenomena, and *pada*, in this context, means "path" or "verses."

The Twin-Verses

*A*ll that we are is the result of what we have thought: it is founded on our thoughts, it is made up of our thoughts. If a man speaks or acts with an evil thought, pain follows him, as the wheel follows the foot of the ox that draws the carriage.

*A*ll that we are is the result of what we have thought: it is founded on our thoughts, it is made up of our thoughts. If a man speaks or acts with a pure thought, happiness follows him, like a shadow that never leaves him.

"He abused me, he beat me, he defeated me, he robbed me"—in those who harbor such thoughts hatred will never cease.

"He abused me, he beat me, he defeated me, he robbed me"—in those who do not harbor such thoughts hatred will cease.

For hatred does not cease by hatred at any time: hatred ceases by love—this is an old rule.

The world does not know that we must all come to an end here; but those who know it, their quarrels cease at once.

He who lives looking for pleasures only, his senses uncontrolled, immoderate in his food, idle, and weak, Mâra, the tempter, will certainly overthrow him, as the wind throws down a weak tree.

He who lives without looking for pleasures, his senses well controlled, moderate in his food, faithful and strong, him Mâra will certainly not overthrow, any more than the wind throws down a rocky mountain.

He who wishes to put on the yellow dress without having cleansed himself from sin, who disregards temperance and truth, is unworthy of the yellow dress.

But he who has cleansed himself from sin, is well grounded in all virtues, and endowed also with temperance and truth, he is indeed worthy of the yellow dress.

They who imagine truth in untruth, and see untruth in truth, never arrive at truth, but follow vain desires.

They who know truth in truth, and untruth in untruth,

arrive at truth, and follow true desires.

As rain breaks through an ill-thatched house,

passion will break through an unreflecting mind.

As rain does not break through a well-thatched

house, passion will not break through

a well-reflecting mind.

The evildoer mourns in this world, and he mourns

in the next; he mourns in both. He mourns and

suffers when he sees the evil of his own work.

The virtuous man delights in this world, and he delights in the next; he delights in both. He delights and rejoices, when he sees the purity of his own work.

The evildoer suffers in this world, and he suffers in the next; he suffers in both. He suffers when he thinks of the evil he has done; he suffers more when going on the evil path.

The virtuous man is happy in this world, and he is happy in the next; he is happy in both. He is happy when he thinks of the good he has done; he is still more happy when going on the good path.

$\mathcal{T}$he thoughtless man, even if he can recite a large portion (of the law), but is not a doer of it, has no share in the priesthood, but is like a cowherd counting the cows of others.

$\mathcal{T}$he follower of the law, even if he can recite only a small portion (of the law), but, having forsaken passion and hatred and foolishness, possesses true knowledge and serenity of mind, he, caring for nothing in this world or that to come, has indeed a share in the priesthood.

On Earnestness

*E*arnestness is the path of immortality (Nirvana),
thoughtlessness the path of death. Those who
are in earnest do not die, those who are
thoughtless are as if dead already.

*H*aving understood this clearly, those who are
advanced in earnestness delight in earnestness, and
rejoice in the knowledge of the Ariyas (the elect).

*T*hese wise people, meditative, steady, always possessed
of strong powers, attain to Nirvana, the highest happiness.

If an earnest person has roused himself,
if he is not forgetful, if his deeds are pure, if he acts
with consideration, if he restrains himself, and lives
according to law—then his glory will increase.

By rousing himself, by earnestness, by restraint
and control, the wise man may make for himself an
island which no flood can overwhelm.

Fools follow after vanity. The wise man keeps
earnestness as his best jewel.

$\mathcal{F}$ollow not after vanity, nor after the enjoyment of love and lust! He who is earnest and meditative, obtains ample joy.

$\mathcal{W}$hen the learned man drives away vanity by earnestness, he, the wise, climbing the terraced heights of wisdom, looks down upon the fools: free from sorrow he looks down upon the sorrowing crowd, as one that stands on a mountain looks down upon them that stand upon the plain.

$\mathcal{E}$arnest among the thoughtless, awake among the sleepers, the wise man advances like a racer, leaving behind the hack.

*B*y earnestness did Maghavan (Indra) rise to the
lordship of the gods. People praise earnestness;
thoughtlessness is always blamed.

A Bhikshu (mendicant) who delights in earnestness,
who looks with fear on thoughtlessness, moves about
like fire, burning all his fetters, small or large.

A Bhikshu (mendicant) who delights in reflection,
who looks with fear on thoughtlessness, cannot fall away
from his perfect state—he is close upon Nirvana.

Thought

As a fletcher makes straight his arrow, a wise man makes straight his trembling and unsteady thought, which is difficult to guard, difficult to hold back.

As a fish taken from his watery home and thrown on dry ground, our thought trembles all over in order to escape the dominion of Mâra, the tempter.

It is good to tame the mind, which is difficult to hold in and flighty, rushing wherever it listeth; a tamed mind brings happiness.

Let the wise man guard his thoughts, for they are difficult to perceive, very artful, and they rush wherever they list: thoughts well guarded bring happiness.

Those who bridle their mind which travels far, moves about alone, is without a body, and hides in the chamber of the heart, will be free from the bonds of Mâra, the tempter.

If a man's faith is unsteady, if he does not know the true law, if his peace of mind is troubled, his knowledge will never be perfect.

If a man's thoughts are not dissipated, if his mind is not perplexed, if he has ceased to think of good or evil, then there is no fear for him while he is watchful.

Knowing that this body is fragile like a jar, and making this thought firm like a fortress, one should attack Mâra, the tempter, with the weapon of knowledge, one should watch him when conquered, and should never rest.

*B*efore long, alas! this body will lie on the earth,

despised, without understanding, like a useless log.

*W*hatever a hater may do to a hater, or an enemy

to an enemy, a wrongly directed mind

will do us greater mischief.

*N*ot a mother, not a father, will do so much,

nor any other relative; a well directed mind

will do us greater service.

The Wise Man

If you see an intelligent man who shows you what is
to be avoided, who administers reproofs, follow that
wise man as you would one who tells of hidden treasure;
it will be better, not worse, for those who follow him.

Let him admonish, let him teach, let him forbid
what is improper!—he will be beloved of the good,
by the bad he will be hated.

Do not have evildoers for friends, do not have
low people for friends: have virtuous people for friends,
have for friends the best of men.

He who drinks in the law lives happily with a
serene mind: the sage rejoices always in the law,
as preached by the elect (Ariyas).

Well-makers lead the water wherever they like;
fletchers bend the arrow; carpenters bend a log of wood;
wise people fashion themselves.

As a solid rock is not shaken by the wind, wise people
falter not amidst blame and praise.

$\mathcal{W}$ise people, after they have listened to the laws,
become serene, like a deep, smooth, and still lake.

$\mathcal{G}$ood men indeed walk warily under all circumstances;
good men speak not out of desire for sensual gratification;
whether touched by happiness or sorrow wise people
never appear elated or depressed.

$\mathcal{I}$f, whether for his own sake, or for the sake of
others, a man wishes neither for a son, nor for
wealth, nor for lordship, and if he does not wish
for his own success by unfair means, then he
is good, wise, and virtuous.

$\mathcal{F}$ew are there among men who arrive at the other shore (become Arhats); the other people here run up and down the shore.

$\mathcal{B}$ut those who, when the law has been well preached to them, follow the law, will pass over the dominion of death, however difficult to cross.

$\mathcal{A}$ wise man should leave the dark state of ordinary life, and follow the bright state of the Bhikshu. After going from his home to a homeless state, he should in his retirement look for enjoyment where there seemed to be no enjoyment. Leaving all pleasures behind, and calling nothing his own, the wise man should purge himself from all the troubles of the mind.

$\mathcal{T}$hose whose mind is well grounded in the (seven) elements of knowledge, who without clinging to anything, rejoice in freedom from attachment, whose appetites have been conquered, and who are full of light, are free even in this world.

The Thousands

*E*ven though a speech be a thousand (words),
but made up of senseless words, one word of sense
is better, which if a man hears, he becomes quiet.

*E*ven though a Gatha (poem) be a thousand (words),
but made up of senseless words, one word of a Gatha
is better, which if a man hears, he becomes quiet.

*T*hough a man recite a hundred Gathas made up
of senseless words, one word of the law is better,
which if a man hears, he becomes quiet.

If one man conquer in battle a thousand times a
thousand men, and if another conquer himself,
he is the greatest of conquerors.

One's own self conquered is better than all other people;
not even a god, a Gandharva, not Mâra with Brahman
could change into defeat the victory of a man who has
vanquished himself, and always lives under restraint.

If a man for a hundred years sacrifice month after month
with a thousand, and if he but for one moment pay homage
to a man whose soul is grounded in true knowledge, better
is that homage than sacrifice for a hundred years.

*I*f a man for a hundred years worship Agni (fire)
in the forest, and if he but for one moment
pay homage to a man whose soul is grounded
in true knowledge, better is that homage
than sacrifice for a hundred years.

*W*hatever a man sacrifice in this world as an offering
or as an oblation for a whole year in order to gain merit,
the whole of it is not worth a quarter; reverence
shown to the righteous is better.

*H*e who always greets and constantly reveres the
aged, four things will increase to him:
life, beauty, happiness, power.

But he who lives a hundred years, vicious and unrestrained, a life of one day is better if a man is virtuous and reflecting.

And he who lives a hundred years, ignorant and unrestrained, a life of one day is better if a man is wise and reflecting.

And he who lives a hundred years, idle and weak, a life of one day is better if a man has attained firm strength.

*A*nd he who lives a hundred years, not seeing
beginning and end, a life of one day is better
if a man sees beginning and end.

*A*nd he who lives a hundred years, not seeing the
immortal place, a life of one day is better if a man
sees the immortal place.

*A*nd he who lives a hundred years, not seeing
the highest law, a life of one day is better
if a man sees the highest law.

Self

$\mathcal{I}$f a man hold himself dear, let him watch himself carefully; during one at least out of the three watches a wise man should be watchful.

$\mathcal{L}$et each man direct himself first to what is proper, then let him teach others; thus a wise man will not suffer.

$\mathcal{I}$f a man make himself as he teaches others to be, then, being himself well subdued, he may subdue (others); one's own self is indeed difficult to subdue.

*S*elf is the lord of self, who else could be the lord? 160

With self well subdued, a man finds a

lord such as few can find.

*T*he evil done by oneself, self-begotten, self-bred, 161

crushes the foolish, as a diamond breaks a precious stone.

*H*e whose wickedness is very great brings himself 162

down to that state where his enemy wishes him

to be, as a creeper does with the tree

which it surrounds.

*B*ad deeds, and deeds hurtful to ourselves, are easy to do; what is beneficial and good, that is very difficult to do.

*T*he foolish man who scorns the rule of the venerable (Arhat), of the elect (Ariya), of the virtuous, and follows false doctrine, he bears fruit to his own destruction, like the fruits of the Katthaka reed.

$\mathcal{B}$y oneself the evil is done, by oneself one suffers;
by oneself evil is left undone, by oneself one is purified.
Purity and impurity (stand and fall) by themselves,
no one can purify another.

$\mathcal{L}$et no one forget his own duty for the sake of another's,
however great; let a man, after he has discerned his own
duty, be always attentive to his duty.

The World

*D*o not follow the evil law! Do not live on in thoughtlessness! Do not follow false doctrine! Be not a friend of the world.

*R*ouse thyself! Do not be idle! Follow the law of virtue! The virtuous rests in bliss in this world and in the next.

*F*ollow the law of virtue; do not follow that of sin. The virtuous rests in bliss in this world and in the next.

Look upon the world as a bubble, look upon it as
a mirage: the king of death does not see him who
thus looks down upon the world.

Come, look at this glittering world, like unto
a royal chariot; the foolish are immersed in it,
but the wise do not touch it.

He who formerly was reckless and afterwards became
sober, brightens up this world, like the moon
when freed from clouds.

*H*e whose evil deeds are covered by good deeds, brightens up this world, like the moon when freed from clouds.

*T*his world is dark, few only can see here; a few only go to heaven, like birds escaped from the net.

*T*he swans go on the path of the sun, they go miraculously through the ether; the wise are led out of this world, when they have conquered Mâra and his train.

If a man has transgressed one law, and
speaks lies, and scoffs at another world,
there is no evil he will not do.

The uncharitable do not go to the world of the
gods; fools only do not praise liberality; a wise man
rejoices in liberality, and through it becomes
blessed in the other world.

Better than sovereignty over the earth, better than
going to heaven, better than lordship over all worlds,
is the reward of Sotapatti, the first step in holiness.

The Buddha (The Awakened)

He whose conquest is not conquered again,
into whose conquest no one in this world enters,
by what track can you lead him, the Awakened,
the Omniscient, the trackless?

He whom no desire with its snares and poisons can lead
astray, by what track can you lead him, the Awakened,
the Omniscient, the trackless?

Even the gods envy those who are awakened and not
forgetful, who are given to meditation, who are wise, and
who delight in the repose of retirement from the world.

$\mathcal{D}$ifficult to obtain is the conception of men, difficult is the life of mortals, difficult is the hearing of the True Law, difficult is the birth of the Awakened (the attainment of Buddhahood).

$\mathcal{N}$ot to commit any sin, to do good, and to purify one's mind, that is the teaching of all the Awakened.

$\mathcal{T}$he Awakened call patience the highest penance, long-suffering the highest Nirvana; for he is not an anchorite (pravragita) who strikes others, he is not an ascetic (sramana) who insults others.

$\mathcal{N}$ot to blame, not to strike, to live restrained under the law, to be moderate in eating, to sleep and sit alone, and to dwell on the highest thoughts—this is the teaching of the Awakened.

$\mathcal{T}$here is no satisfying lusts, even by a shower of gold pieces; he who knows that lusts have a short taste and cause pain, he is wise;

$\mathcal{E}$ven in heavenly pleasures he finds no satisfaction, the disciple who is fully awakened delights only in the destruction of all desires.

$\mathcal{M}$en, driven by fear, go to many a refuge, to mountains and forests, to groves and sacred trees.

$\mathcal{B}$ut that is not a safe refuge, that is not the best refuge; a man is not delivered from all pains after having gone to that refuge.

$\mathcal{H}$e who takes refuge with Buddha, the Law, and the Church; he who, with clear understanding, sees the four holy truths:

Pain, the origin of pain, the destruction of pain, and the eightfold holy way that leads to the quieting of pain.

That is the safe refuge, that is the best refuge; having gone to that refuge, a man is delivered from all pain.

A supernatural person (a Buddha) is not easily found, he is not born everywhere. Wherever such a sage is born, that race prospers.

*H*appy is the arising of the awakened, happy is the

teaching of the True Law, happy is peace in the church,

happy is the devotion of those who are at peace.

*H*e who pays homage to those who deserve homage,

whether the awakened (Buddha) or their disciples, those

who have overcome the host of evils, and crossed the

flood of sorrow, he who pays homage to such as have

found deliverance and know no fear, his merit

can never be measured by anyone.

Happiness

*L*et us live happily then, not hating those who hate us! among men who hate us let us dwell free from hatred!

*L*et us live happily then, free from ailments among the ailing! among men who are ailing let us dwell free from ailments!

*L*et us live happily then, free from greed among the greedy! among men who are greedy let us dwell free from greed!

*L*et us live happily then, though we call nothing our own! We shall be like the bright gods, feeding on happiness!

*V*ictory breeds hatred, for the conquered is unhappy. He who has given up both victory and defeat, he, the contented, is happy.

*T*here is no fire like passion; there is no losing throw like hatred; there is no pain like this body; there is no happiness higher than rest.

*H*unger is the worst of diseases, the body the greatest

of pains; if one knows this truly, that is Nirvana,

the highest happiness.

*H*ealth is the greatest of gifts, contentedness the

best riches; trust is the best of relationships,

Nirvana the highest happiness.

*H*e who has tasted the sweetness of solitude and

tranquility, is free from fear and free from sin,

while he tastes the sweetness of drinking in the law.

The sight of the elect (Arya) is good, to live with them is always happiness; if a man does not see fools, he will be truly happy.

He who walks in the company of fools suffers a long way; company with fools, as with an enemy, is always painful; company with the wise is pleasure, like meeting with kinsfolk.

Therefore, one ought to follow the wise, the intelligent, the learned, the much enduring, the dutiful, the elect; one ought to follow a good and wise man, as the moon follows the path of the stars.

The Just

 man is not just if he carries a matter by violence; no, he who distinguishes both right and wrong, who is learned and leads others, not by violence, but by law and equity, and who is guarded by the law and intelligent, he is called just.

 man is not learned because he talks much; he who is patient, free from hatred and fear, he is called learned.

 man is not a supporter of the law because he talks much; even if a man has learned little, but sees the law bodily, he is a supporter of the law, a man who never neglects the law.

A man is not an elder because his head is gray;
his age may be ripe, but he is called "Old-in-vain."

He in whom there is truth, virtue, love, restraint,
moderation, he who is free from impurity and
is wise, he is called an elder.

An envious, greedy, dishonest man does not become
respectable by means of much talking only,
or by the beauty of his complexion.

*H*e in whom all this is destroyed, and taken out
with the very root, he, when freed from hatred,
is called respectable.

263

*N*ot by tonsure does an undisciplined man
who speaks falsehood become a Samana;
can a man be a Samana who is still held
captive by desire and greediness?

264

*H*e who always quiets the evil, whether small or large,
he is called a Samana (a quiet man), because
he has quieted all evil.

265

A man is not a mendicant (Bhikshu) simply because he asks others for alms; he who adopts the whole law is a Bhikshu, not he who only begs.

He who is above good and evil, who is chaste, who with care passes through the world, he indeed is called a Bhikshu.

A man is not a Muni because he observes silence, if he is foolish and ignorant; but the wise who, taking the balance, chooses the good and avoids evil, he is a Muni, and is a Muni thereby; he who in this world weighs both sides is called a Muni.

A man is not an elect (Ariya) because he injures living creatures; because he has pity on all living creatures, therefore is a man called Ariya.

*N*ot only by discipline and vows, not only by much learning, not by entering into a trance, not by sleeping alone, do I earn the happiness of release which no worldling can know. Bhikshu, be not confident as long as thou hast not attained the extinction of desires.

The Way

*T*he best of ways is the eightfold; the best of truths the four words; the best of virtues passionlessness; the best of men he who has eyes to see.

*T*his is the way, there is no other that leads to the purifying of intelligence. Go on this way! Everything else is the deceit of Mâra, the tempter.

*I*f you go on this way, you will make an end of pain! The way was preached by me, when I had understood the removal of the thorns in the flesh.

*Y*ou yourself must make an effort. The Tathâgatas (Buddhas) are only preachers. The thoughtful who enter the way are freed from the bondage of Mâra.

"*A*ll created things perish," he who knows and sees this becomes passive in pain; this is the way to purity.

"*A*ll created things are grief and pain," he who knows and sees this becomes passive in pain; this is the way that leads to purity.

"All forms are unreal," he who knows and sees this becomes passive in pain; this is the way that leads to purity.

He who does not rouse himself when it is time to rise, who, though young and strong, is full of sloth, whose will and thought are weak, that lazy and idle man will never find the way to knowledge.

Watching his speech, well restrained in mind, let a man never commit any wrong with his body! Let a man but keep these three roads of action clear, and he will achieve the way which is taught by the wise.

*T*hrough zeal knowledge is gained, through lack of zeal knowledge is lost; let a man who knows this double path of gain and loss thus place himself that knowledge may grow.

*C*ut down the whole forest of desires, not a tree only! Danger comes out of the forest of desires. When you have cut down both the forest of desires and its undergrowth, then, Bhikshus, you will be rid of the forest and free of desires!

So long as the love of man towards women, even the
smallest, is not destroyed, so long is his mind in bondage,
as the calf that drinks milk is to its mother.

Cut out the love of self, like an autumn lotus,
with thy hand! Cherish the road of peace.
Nirvana has been shown by Sugata (Buddha).

"Here I shall dwell in the rain, here in winter
and summer," thus the fool meditates,
and does not think of his death.

$\mathcal{D}$eath comes and carries off that man, praised

for his children and flocks, his mind distracted,

as a flood carries off a sleeping village.

$\mathcal{S}$ons are no help, nor a father, nor relations; there is

no help from kinsfolk for one whom death has seized.

$\mathcal{A}$ wise and good man who knows the meaning of this,

should quickly clear the way that leads to Nirvana.

The Brâhmana (Arhat)

*S*top the stream valiantly, drive away the desires,
O Brâhmana! When you have understood the
destruction of all that was made, you will
understand that which was not made.

*I*f the Brâhmana has reached the other shore in
both laws, in restraint and contemplation, all bonds
vanish from him who has obtained knowledge.

*H*e for whom there is neither this nor that shore,
nor both, him, the fearless and unshackled,
I call indeed a Brâhmana.

He who is thoughtful, blameless, settled, dutiful, without passions, and who has attained the highest end, him I call indeed a Brâhmana.

The sun is bright by day, the moon shines by night, the warrior is bright in his armor, the Brâhmana is bright in his meditation; but Buddha, the Awakened, is bright with splendor day and night.

Because a man is rid of evil, therefore he is called Brâhmana; because he walks quietly, therefore he is called Samana; because he has sent away his own impurities, therefore he is called Pravragita (Pabbagita, a pilgrim).

*N*o one should attack a Brâhmana, but no Brâhmana,
if attacked, should let himself fly at his aggressor!
Woe to him who strikes a Brâhmana, more woe to
him who flies at his aggressor!

*I*t advantages a Brâhmana not a little if he holds
his mind back from the pleasures of life; when all
wish to injure has vanished, pain will cease.

*H*im I call indeed a Brâhmana who does not offend
by body, word, or thought, and is controlled
on these three points.

After a man has once understood the law as taught by the Well-awakened (Buddha), let him worship it carefully, as the Brâhmana worships the sacrificial fire.

A man does not become a Brâhmana by his platted hair, by his family, or by birth; in whom there is truth and righteousness, he is blessed, he is a Brâhmana.

What is the use of platted hair, O fool! what of the raiment of goat-skins? Within thee there is ravening, but the outside thou makest clean.

The man who wears dirty raiments, who is emaciated and covered with veins, who lives alone in the forest and meditates, him I call indeed a Brâhmana.

I do not call a man a Brâhmana because of his origin or of his mother. He is indeed arrogant, and he is wealthy: but the poor, who is free from all attachments, him I call indeed a Brâhmana.

Him I call indeed a Brâhmana who has cut all fetters, who never trembles, is independent and unshackled.

Him I call indeed a Brâhmana who has cut the strap and the thong, the chain with all that pertains to it, who has destroyed all obstacles, and is awakened.

Him I call indeed a Brâhmana who, though he has committed no offense, endures reproach, bonds, and stripes, who has endurance for his force, and strength for his army.

Him I call indeed a Brâhmana who is free from anger, dutiful, virtuous, without appetite, who is subdued, and has received his last body.

*H*im I call indeed a Brâhmana who does not cling to sensual pleasures, like water on a lotus leaf, like a mustard seed on the point of a needle.

*H*im I call indeed a Brâhmana who, even here, knows the end of his own suffering, has put down his burden, and is unshackled.

*H*im I call indeed a Brâhmana whose knowledge is deep, who possesses wisdom, who knows the right way and the wrong, and has attained the highest end.

Him I call indeed a Brâhmana who keeps aloof both from laymen and from mendicants, who frequents no houses, and has but few desires.

Him I call indeed a Brâhmana who finds no fault with other beings, whether feeble or strong, and does not kill nor cause slaughter.

Him I call indeed a Brâhmana who is tolerant with the intolerant, mild with the violent, and free from passion among the passionate.

$\mathcal{H}$im I call indeed a Brâhmana from whom anger
and hatred, pride and envy have dropped like a
mustard seed from the point of a needle.

$\mathcal{H}$im I call indeed a Brâhmana who utters true
speech, instructive and free from harshness,
so that he offend no one.

$\mathcal{H}$im I call indeed a Brâhmana who takes nothing
in the world that is not given him, be it long or short,
small or large, good or bad.

*H*im I call indeed a Brâhmana who fosters no desires for this world or for the next, has no inclinations, and is unshackled.

*H*im I call indeed a Brâhmana who has no interests, and when he has understood the truth, does not say How, how? and who has reached the depth of the Immortal.

*H*im I call indeed a Brâhmana who in this world has risen above good and evil, above the bondage of both, free from grief, from sin, and from impurity.

*H*im I call indeed a Brâhmana who is bright
like the moon, pure, serene, undisturbed,
and in whom all gaiety is extinct.

*H*im I call indeed a Brâhmana who has traversed
this miry road, the impassable world and its vanity,
who has gone through, and reached the other shore,
is thoughtful, steadfast, free from doubts,
free from attachment, and content.

*H*im I call indeed a Brâhmana who in this world,
having abandoned all desires, travels about without
a home, and in whom all concupiscence is extinct.

*H*im I call indeed a Brâhmana who, having abandoned all longings, travels about without a home, and in whom all covetousness is extinct.

*H*im I call indeed a Brâhmana who, after leaving all bondage to men, has risen above all bondage to the gods, and is free from all and every bondage.

*H*im I call indeed a Brâhmana who has left what gives pleasure and what gives pain, who is cold, and free from all germs (of renewed life), the hero who has conquered all the worlds.

*H*im I call indeed a Brâhmana who knows the destruction and the return of beings everywhere, who is free from bondage, welfaring (Sugata), and awakened (Buddha).

*H*im I call indeed a Brâhmana whose path the gods do not know, nor spirits (Gandharvas), nor men, whose passions are extinct, and who is an Arhat (venerable).

*H*im I call indeed a Brâhmana who calls nothing his own, whether it be before, behind, or between, who is poor, and free from the love of the world.

*H*im I call indeed a Brâhmana, the manly, the noble, the hero, the great sage, the conqueror, the indifferent, the accomplished, the awakened.

*H*im I call indeed a Brâhmana who knows his former abodes, who sees heaven and hell, has reached the end of births, is perfect in knowledge, a sage, and whose perfections are all perfect.

MORE BUDDHIST
WISDOM

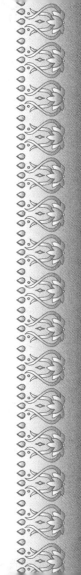

*Y*ou are perfect as you are, and could use a little work.

—Shunryu Suzuki, *Zen Mind, Beginner's Mind*

*N*othing worthwhile is achieved overnight.

—Bhante Henepola Gunaratana,
Mindfulness in Plain English

*W*hat you think is a problem comes from your own mind, what you think is joyful comes from your own mind. Your happiness does not depend on anything external.

—Lama Zopa Rinpoche,
Transforming Problems into Happiness

If you never try, you can never be successful,

but if you try, you might surprise yourself.

—Lama Thubten Yeshe, *The Bliss of Inner Fire*

If we're looking for outer conditions to bring us

contentment, we're looking in vain.

—Ayya Khema, *Be an Island*

Compassion is the best healer.

—Lama Zopa Rinpoche, *Ultimate Healing*

If you're feeling helpless,

help someone.

—Aung San Suu Kyi,
winner, Nobel Peace Prize (1991)

$\mathcal{T}$he four basic ingredients for success are: you must have the will to want something; you must have the right kind of attitude; you must have perseverance, and then you must have wisdom. Then you combine these four and then you get to where you want to get to.

—Aung San Suu Kyi

$\mathcal{D}$espite its practical uses, the true context of meditation is spiritual life.

—Daniel Goleman, *The Meditative Mind: The Varieties of Meditative Experience*

The only real prison is fear, and the only real freedom

is freedom from fear.

—Aung San Suu Kyi

Such transcendental states seem to be the seeds

of spiritual life, and they have been experienced by the

founders and early followers of every world religion.

Moses receiving the Ten Commandments, Jesus'

forty-day vigil in the wilderness, Allah's desert vision, and

Buddha's enlightenment under the Bo Tree all bespeak

extraordinary states of consciousness.

—Daniel Goleman, *The Meditative Mind:*
The Varieties of Meditative Experience

*M*any people are afraid to empty their minds lest they may plunge into the Void. They do not know that their own Mind is the Void. The ignorant eschew phenomena but not thought; the wise eschew thought but not phenomena.

—Huang Po, *Zen Teaching of Huang Po*

*O*vercoming attachment does not mean becoming cold
and indifferent. On the contrary, it means learning to have
relaxed control over our mind through understanding
the real causes of happiness and fulfillment, and this
enables us to enjoy life more and suffer less.

—Kathleen McDonald, *How to Meditate*

*D*estruction of the nonexistent is easy;
no attachment to the existent is hard.

—Adept Godrakpa, *In Hermit of Go Cliffs*

*R*ealization comes naturally thorough the practice

of surrendering.

—Jae Woong Kim, *Polishing the Diamond*

*D*on't cling to anything and don't reject anything.

Let come what comes, and accommodate

yourself to that, whatever it is.

—Bhante Henepola Gunaratana,
Mindfulness in Plain English

In the beginner's mind there are many possibilities; in the expert's mind there are few.

—Shunryu Suzuki, *Zen Mind, Beginner's Mind*

*Y*ou have to be careful not to criticize or fight the mind, since it is normal to think, hear sounds, and feel sensations. The trick is not to grasp or reject them. Just leave them alone and let them come and go lightly.

—Martine Batchelor, *Meditation for Life*

*L*et go. Learn to flow with all the changes that come up. Loosen up and relax.

—Bhante Henepola Gunaratana,
Mindfulness in Plain English

Accept everything that arises. Accept your
feelings, even the ones you wish you did not have.
Accept your experiences, even the ones you hate.
Don't condemn yourself for having human flaws and failings.
Learn to see all the phenomena in the mind
as being perfectly natural and understandable.
—Bhante Henepola Gunaratana,
Mindfulness in Plain English

$\mathcal{I}$f we find our minds have become agitated, the antidote is to relax more deeply. Relax away the effort that is going into sustaining our conceptual or emotional turbulence.

—B. Alan Wallace, *Tibetan Buddhism from the Ground Up*

If your mind is empty, it is always ready

for anything; it is open to everything.

—Shunryu Suzuki, *Zen Mind, Beginner's Mind*

Mindfulness is never boring.

—Bhante Henepola Gunaratana,

Mindfulness in Plain English

$\mathcal{N}$onattachment doesn't mean that you get rid of your spouse. It means you free yourself from wrong views about yourself and your spouse. Then you find that there's love there, but it's not attached. It's not distorting, clinging, and grasping.

—Ajahn Sumedho, *The Mind and the Way*

$\mathcal{T}$he purpose of studying Buddhism is not to study Buddhism, but to study ourselves.

—Shunryu Suzuki, *Zen Mind, Beginner's Mind*

In order to recognize our self-image,
we can no longer identify with it.
In other words, we have to learn
how to objectify our own
mental processes.

—Matthew Flickstein, *Journey to the Center*

$\mathcal{U}$nless we have the determination to increase

our mindfulness from moment to moment,

we will easily forget to practice it.

—Ayya Khema, *Be an Island*

$\mathcal{E}$very day we are engaged in a miracle which we

don't even recognize: a blue sky, white clouds,

green leaves, the black, curious eyes of a

child—our own two eyes. All is a miracle.

—Thich Nhat Hanh, *Miracle of Mindfulness*

$\mathcal{W}$alk as if you are kissing the Earth with your feet.

—Thich Nhat Hanh, *Peace Is Every Step:
The Path of Mindfulness in Everyday Life*

$\mathcal{I}$ like to walk alone on country paths, rice plants and wild grasses on both sides, putting each foot down on the earth in mindfulness, knowing that I walk on the wondrous earth. In such moments, existence is a miraculous and mysterious reality.

—Thich Nhat Hanh, *Miracle of Mindfulness*

$\mathcal{W}$hen you are having a bad time, examine that badness, observe it mindfully, study the phenomenon, and learn its mechanics.

—Bhante Henepola Gunaratana,
Mindfulness in Plain English

Everything is as it is. It has no name other than the name
we give it. It is we who call it something; we give it value.
We say this thing is good or it's bad, but in itself,
the thing is only as it is. It's not absolute; it's just as it is.
People are just as they are.

—Ajahn Sumedho, *The Mind and the Way*

As a result of interrelatedness and interdependency,
every expression of energy, including our thoughts
and intentions, ultimately touches and
affects everything else.

—Matthew Flickstein, *Journey to the Center*

Half the spiritual life consists in remembering what we are up against and where we are going.

—Ayya Khema, *When the Iron Eagle Flies*

*U*nless we practice loving feelings toward everyone
we meet, day in, day out, we're missing out on the most
joyous part of life. If we can actually open our hearts,
there's no difficulty in being happy.

—Ayya Khema, *Be an Island*

*T*hinking of human beings alone is a bit narrow.
To consider that all sentient beings in the universe
have been our mother at some point in time
opens a space of compassion.

—Dalai Lama, *Imagine All the People*

*Y*ou have always been one with the Buddha,
so do not pretend you can *attain* to this oneness
by various practices.

—Huang Po, *Zen Teaching of Huang Po*

*U*nconditional love is an expression of love that is
not based upon pleasant feelings. It is instead unlimited.
Anyone who meets an individual with unconditional
love can experience its presence, and the one who
expresses it becomes a loving person.

—Mathew Flickstein, *Journey to the Center*

*D*esires achieved increase thirst
like salt water.

—Milarepa, *Drinking the Mountain Stream*,
translated by Lama Kunga Rinpoche & Brian Cutillo

*E*ventually we will find (mostly in retrospect, of course)

that we can be very grateful to those people who

have made life most difficult for us.

—Ayya Khema, *When the Iron Eagle Flies*

*T*o be attached to one's own happiness

is a barrier to the true and perfect path.

To cherish other is the source

of every admirable quality known.

—Tsongkhapa,
The Splendor of an Autumn Moon

$\mathcal{I}$t is very important that you do not compare your actions to your partner's or judge your partner's behavior as unskillful. Rather, focus on your own actions and take responsibility for them. Recall those times when you looked into your partner's eyes and saw the pain you caused. Remind yourself that you have caused this person you love to suffer. If you can admit your own faults, if you can see how hurtful your actions were and tap into a sense of concern for your partner's well-being, then compassion and loving-friendliness will flow.

—Bhante Henepola Gunaratana,
Eight Mindful Steps to Happiness

*L*oving others does not mean that
we should forget ourselves.

—His Holiness the Dalai Lama,
Imagine All the People

The Buddha compared people to four kinds of clay vessels. One type of vessel has holes in the bottom. We can pour in as much water as we like and it runs right out. When this type of person hears the Dharma, it goes in one ear and out the other. The second type of vessel has cracks. Though we pour in the Dharma, it seeps out slowly until the vessel is empty again. The third vessel is full to the brim with stale water—views and opinions. One can't pour anything new in, everything is already known. The only useful vessel is the fourth, without holes or cracks and totally empty.

—Ayya Khema, *Be an Island*

There are times I think I am not
sure of something which
I absolutely know.

—Mongkut, King of Siam, a Buddhist monk
before becoming the King portrayed
in *The King and I*

$\mathcal{H}$ow much of your life do you spend

looking forward to being somewhere else?

—Matthew Flickstein, *Journey to the Center*

Happiness is about one's outlook on life, and
Buddhist values help people appreciate and focus
on what they have instead of what they do not have.
Values such as compassion and respect foster
greater social interaction.

—Karma Tshiteem, Bhutan's Secretary of GNH
(Gross National Happiness)

Acknowledgments

Thanks to all the temples, books, and Buddhists who have helped me learn, to sterling Senior Editor Andrea Rotondo at Sterling Publishing for guiding the book and selecting the *Dhammapada* verses, to Alexander Craig for curating the quotes about Buddhism, to Mom and Dad always, and to those dear ones who have brought Buddhist and/or meditation insights into my life: Teressa Asencia, Eugene Bashe, Denton and Kathy Ferrell, Paul Kaufman, Toshimi Kawashima, the priest of the Mitahora Temple, Sri Hari R Moss, the abiding Moonbow writers, Kay Mouradian, Bonnie Olson, Alicia and Frank Rowe, and Kathy Spielman.